⊖ An Observer's

Making Clothes

Pressing

Gerald Marshall Hall

Illustrations by Barbara Firth

FREDERICK WARNE

Published by Frederick Warne (Publishers) Ltd., 1982
© Frederick Warne (Publishers) Ltd, 1982

For my students past, present and future

Imperial and metric measurements are used throughout the book. Choose either the metric or imperial system and stick to it throughout each project—changing from one system to the other will lead to inaccuracy and mistakes.

ISBN 07232 2890 6

Filmset and printed in Great Britain
by BAS Printers Limited, Over Wallop, Hampshire

Contents

	page
Introduction	5

Phase 1. Press aids   7
Iron. Press board. Pressing cloths. Dabber. Tailor's donkey. Tailor's ham. Press pad. Press roll. Banger. Dowel rod. Knitting needle. Preparing your press board for pressing. Tailor's tips 1–9

Phase 2. Testing   19
Heat test. Moisture tests, Fabric shrinkage. Pre-shrinking. Test pressing. Tailor's tips 10–13

Phase 3. Under pressing   30
Under pressing as you go. Curved seams and darts. Gathered areas. Pleats and design detail. Plain sleeve heads

Phase 4. Layering   36
Hems. Necklines. Neckline and armhole facings. Collars. Lapels and front edges. Layering seams before top stitching. Using the iron when layering edges. Layering iron-on interfacings. Tailor's tips 14–16

Phase 5. Top pressing   45
Tacking edges in preparation. A protective press cloth. Press surfaces. Methods of top pressing. Sequences of top pressing. Tailor's tips 17–18

Phase 6. Pressing off 50

Phase 7. Difficult and unusual fabrics 52
Pile fabrics. Short pile fabrics. Long pile fabrics. Heavy fabrics. Thin fabrics. Tailor's tips 19–23

Phase 8. Other use for press aids 62
Tailor's ham. Tailor's donkey

Introduction

'*Dashing away with the smoothing iron she stole my heart away.*'

As the old song suggests, ironing is for smoothing out wrinkles and creases in garments and pieces of fabric which have gone through a hand or machine laundering process.

On the contrary we cannot dash with pressing. It does exactly what it says, it flattens, or sets seams and darts open or to one side, creases edges such as hems, facings, neck and collar edges. It requires an iron of reasonable weight and heat together with protective press cloths which can be used dry or damp depending on the texture and content of the fabric.

That invisible label attached to a garment which reads *home made* need not be there if pressing is carried out with thought and care, and the help of a few simple press aids. Indeed, 'invisible' should be the key word to good pressing; seam allowances and edges being firmed in such a manner as to appear not to be there.

For this reason it is suggested that you buy an extra 30 cm of your chosen fabric to try out the reactions of the cloth to all the sewing and pressing techniques before you begin to cut out and make your clothes.

You may have a piece of material bought long ago and cannot remember what it is made of—a dress or skirt length that may have been a present, or a remnant bought at a market stall—or maybe in the hustle and bustle of the sales you forgot to find out. This is not unusual, after all you were attracted to the material in the first place by its colour, looks and texture.

This book is written to help you answer such questions as:

'Will this fabric need a hot iron?'; 'should I use a damp press cloth, and if so, how damp will it need to be?'

It will also help you to eliminate that lumpy hem or collar edge and show you how to avoid those strained and tortuous seams.

Phase 1
Press Aids

Pressing equipment need not be an expensive part of your dressmaking. Most of the press aids used in this book can be made easily and the materials for making them found in good department stores and offcut bins in woodshops.

The final section describes how some of this equipment can be invaluable in helping you to sew your clothes, so a really useful set of press aids at your fingertips is a necessity.

Talking of fingertips, we have a set of press aids ready made and close to hand! Put them to good use. I have often jokingly said to my students that they should not worry if a finger gets burnt as they have others to use, but seriously, you could wear an old thin leather glove or the fingers cut from a glove to protect your digits when your iron needs to be close to hand.

The iron

This hard-worked piece of equipment needs to be the best you can afford and must be kept in good condition. A domestic iron weighing approximately 2 kg ($4\frac{1}{2}$ lb) fitted with a thermostat control will enable you to press all your work to a high standard.

Steam irons Steam irons are a boon these days in helping you to dash through your laundry in no time at all and of course can be used for some of the steamier techniques described in this book.

If you have watched a potter or sculptor at work with clay you will have noticed how carefully he moulds and shapes his work and how, when needed, he either carefully applies a little water or splashes lots of water all over his creation, always knowing exactly the right amount to use at the right moment. A similar method is used when pressing so it is suggested that you use a plain domestic iron in unison with damp and dry rags to ensure complete control over your creation.

1 Make sure that the iron is wired correctly.
2 Inspect it at regular intervals for worn flex and loose wires.
3 The base of the iron should be clean at all times—a dirty iron can cause stained or scorched fabrics.

CLEANING YOUR IRON

1 Unplug the iron and clean off any marks with a non-scratch bath or sink cream cleanser.
2 Wipe off the cleanser with a damp cloth. DO NOT immerse the iron in water.
3 Dry the iron's surface with a piece of absorbent kitchen paper.
4 Plug in the iron and set the thermostat control to the lowest heat setting.
5 Rub a white household candle over the base of the warm iron to smear a thin film of wax over its surface.
6 Rub the iron on a piece of absorbent paper to remove excess wax, leaving a clean surface that will remain dirt free for quite a time.

Press board

A press board can be made from a piece of 2.5 cm (1 in) thick blockboard measuring approximately 1 m × 1 m (36 × 36 in). To ensure there are no rough edges to snag your fabric, sandpaper the edges smooth or cover them with sticky tape.

Use the press board on top of a table to give a firm surface for pressing large areas.

1 It will support your press aids whilst in use, allowing the part of the garment not being pressed to rest comfortably to one side of your press aid.
2 It doubles up as an extra work surface.
3 It can be stored easily under a bed or behind a door.

PRESS BOARD COVER

An old matted blanket will make an excellent pressing surface.
Use in one, two or three thicknesses to suit the pressing in hand. Its surface will singe easily so protect it with a piece of cotton sheeting or a piece of tailor's linen canvas.

Pressing cloths

These need to be of good quality. They are used to protect your garment from the heat of the iron and yet allow heat and steam to penetrate through to mould the seams and darts into shape.

THE DAMP RAG—DAMP PRESSING

An old but firmly woven linen tea towel or a 50 cm ($\frac{1}{2}$ yd) piece of tailor's linen canvas will make an excellent moisture-retaining damp rag.

Use for all pressing-with-moisture techniques.

1   Soak the tailor's canvas overnight to loosen the surface dressing and then wash out.
2   Keep your damp rag away from delicate fabrics as these tend to water stain.

THE DRY PRESS CLOTH—DRY PRESSING

Two types of protective press cloths will be sufficient for most dry pressing techniques.

1   A piece of woollen worsted.
Use to firm, or set, the pressed area after the damp rag has been used.
2   A piece of pure silk or cotton twill.
Use to protect garments when dry-pressing.

Look for these materials at remnant counters or use discarded trousers, silk shirts or an unwanted silk head scarf. You might easily find these at jumble sales.

The dabber—moisture spreader

A dabber is a cigar-shaped roll of absorbent cloth such as cotton, woollen worsted or flannel, tightly rolled up and sewn to form a 2.5 cm (1 in) thick tube.

Use to transfer small amounts of moisture to seams, darts and difficult-to-get-at areas when pressing on the wrong side of the garment with the bare iron.

TO MAKE THE DABBER (Figure 1)

1   Cut an oblong piece of absorbent cloth (cotton, woollen worsted or flannel).
2   Roll up the cloth firmly from one end making a tight, cigar-shaped roll.

3 Whip stitch the end of the roll to the roll itself with firm stitches and sew a loop of tape at one end to hang the dabber up when not in use.

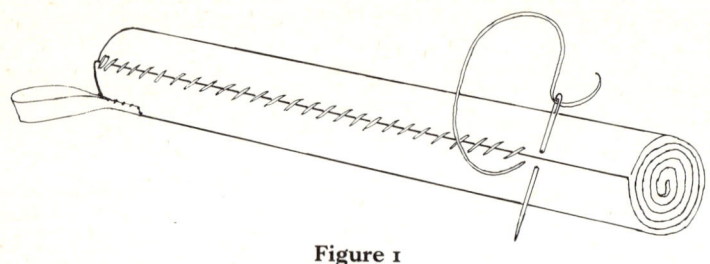

Figure 1

Tailor's donkey—large wooden sleeve board

Sometimes called a duplex board, this is used as a miniature ironing board, resting on top of your press board. When 'burdened' with the press cushion, or some other press aid, it is often called a *donkey*, and in this book I refer to it as a *tailor's donkey*. It is quite an expensive article to buy but can be made from 2 cm (¾ in) thick wood by following the simple graph pattern in Figure 2. The finished board will look like Figure 3 and will need a cover.

TO MAKE A COVER FOR THE TAILOR'S DONKEY (Figure 4)

Materials to use   A thin blanket, flannel, woollen worsted or smoothly woven tweed. An additional protective cover can be made from tailor's linen canvas.

1 Lay your donkey top side down on a piece of paper, draw round the shape and add about 6.5 cm (2½ in) to the outer edge for turn-under and hem.

2 Cut this shape out in fabric. Turn in 2.5 cm (1 in) all round and machine stitch to form a channel hem, leaving a small opening at the broad end of the shape.

3 Thread strong string or cord through this channel making sure that you leave quite a bit of string at either end for easier tying.

4 Place your cover over the donkey and draw up the string tightly. Using the dividing block as an anchor point, wind the string round this point several times before tying off.

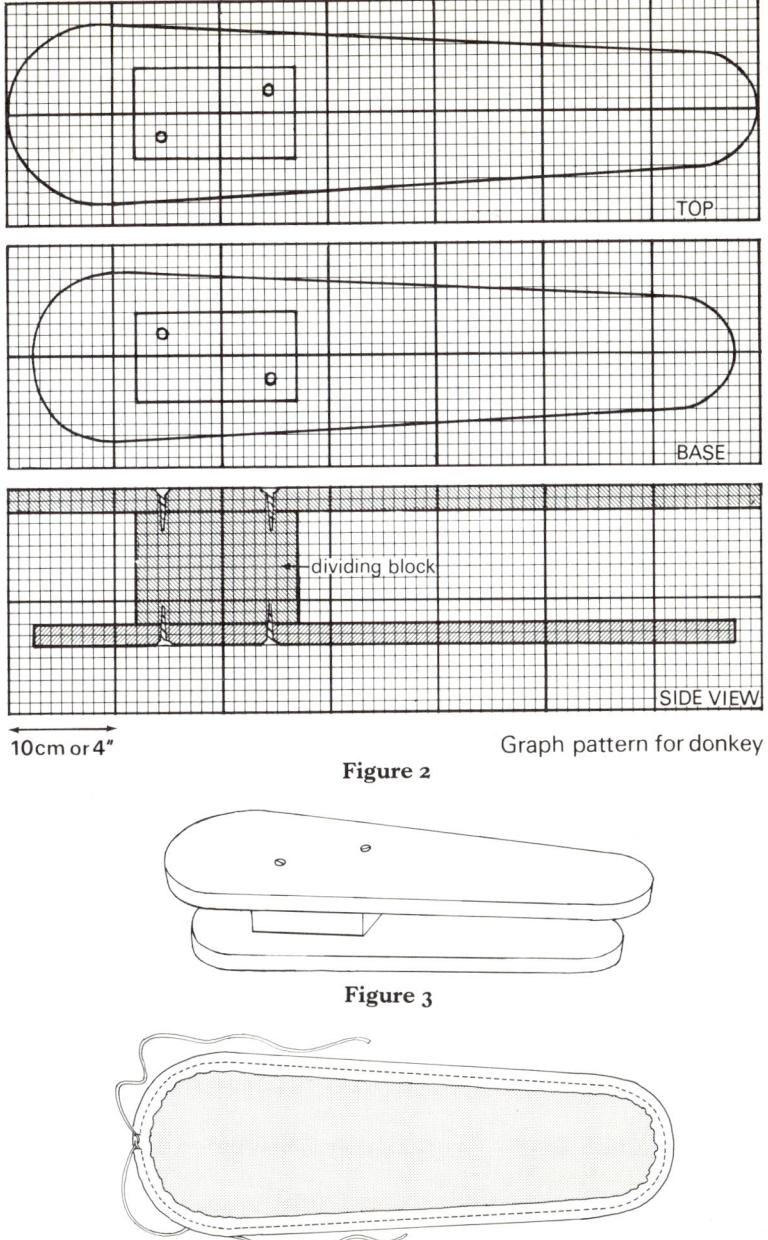

10cm or 4"

Graph pattern for donkey

Figure 2

Figure 3

Figure 4

Tailor's ham—press cushion

This is a firm, but not hard, egg-shaped pad stuffed with chopped up rags or a mixture of scissored rags and kapoc.

Use
1   When pressing and moulding darts into shape.
2   When shrinking away fullness at the end of dart areas such as bust points and hips.
3   When pressing open delicate fabrics and when coaxing stubborn fabrics into place.
4   When shrinking away ease in sleeve heads and other 'eased in' areas mentioned in paper patterns.
5   'Loaded' on top of the tailor's donkey. This invaluable press aid raises up and isolates the part to be pressed.

To make a tailor's ham (Figure 5)
1   From a 50 cm ($\frac{1}{2}$ yd) piece of 90 cm (36 in) wide, closely woven calico or feather-proofed cotton, cut two egg-shaped pieces as shown in the diagram.
2   Machine stitch the two pieces together leaving an opening on the lip side large enough for your hand to pass through.
3   Machine stitch a second strengthening row 6 mm ($\frac{1}{4}$ in) outside the first row of stitching.
4   Turn out the pad to the right side and stuff with scissored rags or a mixture of chopped rags and kapoc.
5   Continue filling until very firm and egg shaped. Turn in the lip ends and whip stitch these open ends firmly together.

Tailor's tips 1–4
1   Damping the stuffing slightly will help you get a firmer filling.
2   When nearly full grab hold of the open sides and bang the pad on a hard surface to distribute the filling evenly. You will find by doing this there will be lots more room for further stuffing.
3   Finish off by drying in an airing cupboard or some other warm place.
4   At the first signs of wear, re-cover the tailor's ham, leaving the original cover intact.

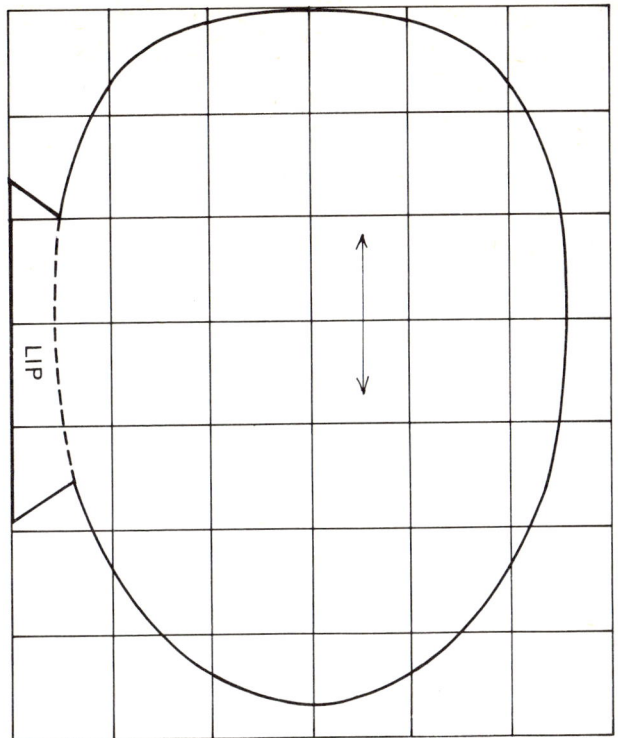

HAM: each square = 6cm or $2\frac{1}{2}''$ sq.
SMALL PAD: "   " = 3cm or $1\frac{1}{4}''$ sq.

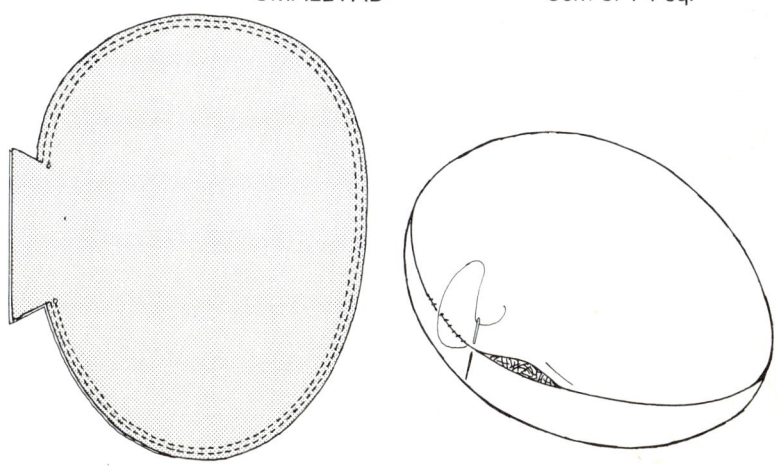

Figure 5

Press pad

A press pad is a half-size version of the tailor's ham which is used in the hand when pressing inside small or difficult-to-get-at areas.

Use

1   When pressing sleeve ends.
2   When pressing collar bands, neck edges etc.
3   When pressing pockets and cuffs.
4   As a tailor's ham when making small children's clothes.

TO MAKE A PRESS PAD

Make a press pad in a similar manner to the tailor's ham. Using the off-cuts from the tailor's ham, *halve* the measurements of the diagram for the tailor's ham for a half-scale version.

Press roll (Figure 6)

A press roll can be made from a stout cardboard roll, a discarded wooden rolling pin or a half-used, unwanted roll of wallpaper covered with a closely fitting tube of woollen worsted.

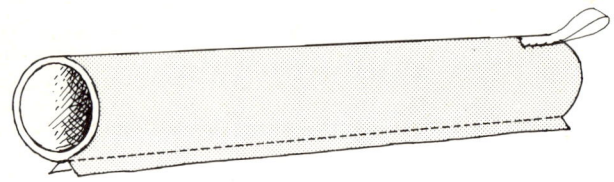

Figure 6

Use

1   On top of the donkey when pressing seams open where there is the possibility of seam impressions showing through to the right side of the garment.
2   For threading through tubes of fabric such as tie collars, wide belts, sashes and tight sleeves when pressing the seams open.

TO MAKE A PRESS ROLL COVER

1   Measure the length and circumference of the roll and add 2 cm ($\frac{3}{4}$ in) to the circumference measurement for seam allowances.
2   Cut out an oblong piece of flannel or woollen worsted to these measurements.
3   Fold to form a long tube and machine stitch along its length leaving 9 mm ($\frac{3}{8}$ in) seam allowance.

4 With these seam allowances on the outside, pull the fabric tube over one end of the press roll until it covers it.

5 Sew a loop of tape at one end for hanging the press roll up when not in use.

Note   The seam allowances are left on the outside of the roll to prevent the tube from rolling about when in use.

Banger—Pounding block or clapper

This is a smoothly finished block of hardwood approximately 8 × 8 × 18 cm (3 × 3 × 7 in).

Use

1 To flatten the hems and edges of garments whilst still warm from the iron.

2 *Only* on very heavy fabrics that have no surface design.

MINI BANGER (Figure 7)

To make this mini version of the banger tape the pages of an unwanted paperback book together with adhesive tape and cover with an envelope of woollen worsted or flannel.

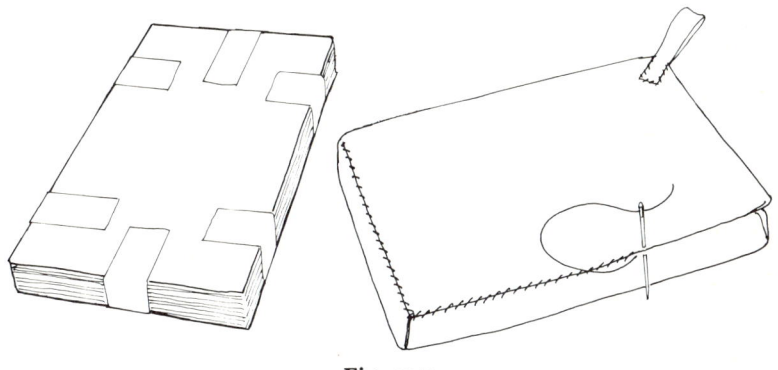

Figure 7

Use

1 As a gentler version of the banger, or pounding block, for flattening, and removing steam quickly from hems and edges on all but the heaviest of fabrics.

2 To insert in to sleeve ends, pockets and similar openings to isolate the part you are pressing.

Dowel rod

This is a wooden curtail rail approximately 12 mm ($\frac{1}{2}$ in) diameter and 50 cm (19 in) long.

Be sure to smooth the ends of the rod with sandpaper so that they do not snag your fabric.

Use

1   For threading through narrow tubes of fabric for belts and rouleau so that when pressing the seam open you do not press the edge of the tube.

2   To help turn out these tubes to the right side of the fabric.

Large wooden knitting needle

Use

1   In a similar manner to the dowel rod when working on even smaller tubes of fabric.

2   For getting in to the pointed ends of collars, lapels and similar angles so that these difficult corners can be lightly pressed open to help them to turn out more easily.

3   The end of the knitting needle to ease out corners when turning them to the right side.

Preparing your press board for pressing (Figure 8)

The press board is the most important press aid, so take time and care to set it up in an organized manner. By following the suggestions below you will be able to look forward to trouble-free pressing in all your dressmaking projects.

1   Place a table in a well-lit area close to an electric point and lay your press board on top of it.

2   Lay your pressing blanket on the board and protect its surface with a piece of cotton sheeting or tailor's linen.

3   Place your press aids towards the back of the table ready to be brought forward when needed.

4   Half fill a container, such as a large, plastic, ice-cream box, with fresh water and place to one side of the board. Alongside it have a second container in which you can keep your damp rag safely stored away from materials that could be stained or damaged by moisture contact.

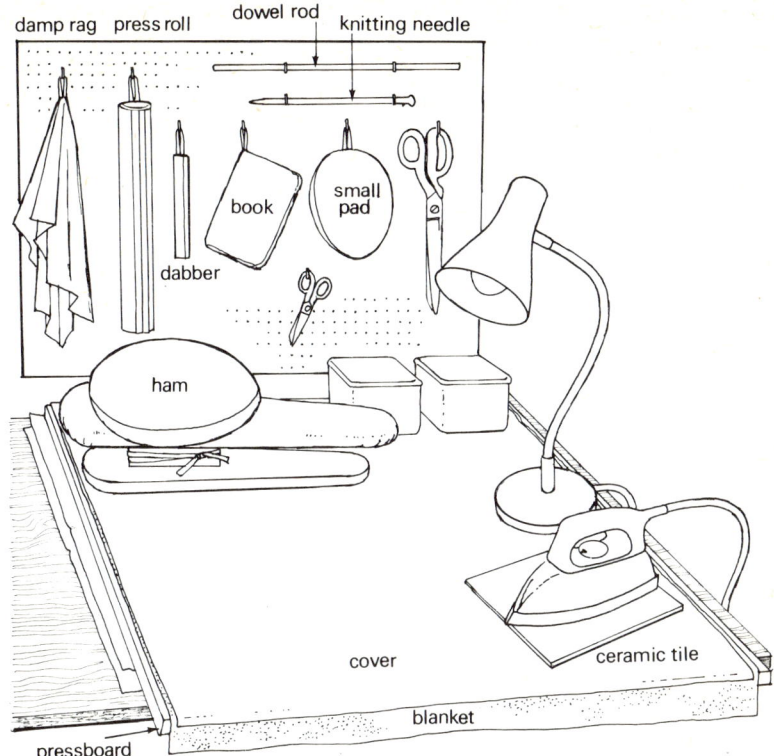

Figure 8

5   Soak one quarter of your damp rag in the water; wring it out on the remaining three quarters. This will give you the correct moisture content for most pressing-with-moisture operations.

6   Soak one end of the dabber in the water and squeeze out the excess water. Keep your dabber together with your damp rag safely in the plastic container.

Tailor's tips 5–9

5   Prevent your board from marking the table you have placed it on by placing several thicknesses of newspaper underneath the board.

6   If you have a sewing room you could mount a pegboard above your press table, so that much of your equipment can be hung up out of the way when not in use.

7 An office desk lamp can be a great help in directing extra light on to your work.

8 A ceramic tile makes a good iron stand.

9 Slapping your damp rag on your pressboard, rather like a window cleaner slaps his wash leather, will give you an evenly distributed damp rag.

Phase 2
Testing

When you embark on making your own clothes a myriad weaves, textures and fibres await your scissors. From the vast range of available fabrics you will need to know how the one you have chosen to make into a garment reacts to heat from the iron and moisture from the dabber and damp rag.

Apart from all pile and nap-surfaced fabrics such as velvet, velveteen, velour, needlecord and corduroy, which are all dealt with in the section on 'unusual and difficult fabrics', there is a way of eliminating all uncertainty when pressing your garment.

If you have been able to buy an extra piece of fabric, as was suggested earlier, or can spare a reasonably sized piece of your cloth as a sample, you are now ready for a test run to find out which of the three following pressing techniques is best suited to your material.

1 *The damp-dabber and damp-rag method* for all fabrics that are not harmed by moisture

2 *The dry-press method* for materials that are affected by moisture in such a way as to cause water marking and or colour bleeding

3 *The dry-press and damp-dabber method* for light and medium-weight fabrics that could be harmed by moisture and yet need extra coaxing into place

Before you decide on the correct method you must discover the heat setting best suited to your fabric and the basic reactions of your test piece to moisture.

Heat test

HOW HOT DOES THE IRON NEED TO BE?

1 Switch on the iron and turn the thermostat (heat control) to its lowest setting (light on).
2 When this temperature is reached (light off) try pressing a crease into one corner of your test piece using the bare iron on the wrong side of the fabric. Usually only the thinnest materials are affected by such a low heat setting so, unless this heat makes an impression on your fabric, move on up the heat scale marked on the iron until you find a temperature that creases your sample easily without using undue pressure with the iron.
3 Make a note of the heat setting best suited to your fabric.
4 Keep one half of your test piece to use as a protective press cloth when finally pressing off your finished garment.

YOUR IRON IS TOO HOT IF:

1 a sticky or dragging sensation is felt when placing the iron on the fabric.
2 there is an acrid smell when pressing man-made fibres or a smell of singeing (burnt feathers) when pressing natural fabrics.
3 your fabric shrivels up or becomes brittle when it comes into contact with the iron.

A dirty iron can also cause these problems! Be sure to check that the iron is clean.

Tailor's tip 10

Keep the spare test piece in your handbag for easy reference when choosing or matching accessories, buttons, zip fasteners, sewing threads and linings.

Moisture tests

It is advisable to test your material's response to moisture before you start to sew. Look out for signs of water marking, colour bleeding and shrinking.

WATER MARKING

In the medium and light-weight range of fabrics there are quite a number that are affected by water marks. These marks are very unsightly and look as if something has been spilt over the garment.

To test for water marks:

1   With the iron at the heat setting best suited to your sample piece, lay your sample face (right side) down and smear a film of water over one corner with your moistened dabber.
2   Place the bare iron on top to dry off the moisture.
3   Inspect the surface on both sides for stains or discoloration.
4   If apparent, you will need to use the DRY-PRESS method or possibly the DRY-PRESS AND DAMP-DABBER technique.
5   If free of marks the DAMP-DABBER AND DAMP-RAG technique can be used.

COLOUR BLEEDING

Colour bleeding caused by unfast dyes is still apparent in some fabrics including braids and trimmings. It is wise to be aware of the possibility of the colours running especially when mixing two fabrics, or a fabric and braid, together in one garment.

To test for colour bleeding:

1   With the iron at a comfortable heat setting lay your sample piece of fabric, face (right side) down on to a piece of white fabric such as an old handkerchief or piece of cotton sheeting.
2   Smear a film of water with the dabber on to the test fabric or braid and press with the bare iron until dry.
3   If no dye is transferred on to the white cotton, your material or trimming is reasonably fast dyed and can be pressed with the DAMP-DABBER AND DAMP-RAG METHOD.
4   If the colour runs the DRY-PRESS METHOD must be used.
5   After-care will mean washing the garment separately or dry cleaning if fabrics or fabrics and trimmings are mixed.

FABRIC SHRINKAGE

Most fabrics are pre-shrunk these days, but even so, it is wise to test press for possible shrinkage and to bear in mind the following:

Does shrinkage matter?

1   If the garment you are making is fairly loose a small amount of shrinkage would hardly be noticed.
2   But if that close fitting blouse or that narrow skirt you are planning to make shrinks after laundering or dry cleaning you may need to get the diet sheet out.

What are the signs of shrinkage (Figure 9)
1   Your fabric shrinks if a bubbled or rippled effect appears on either side of the pressed area.
2   These signs can occur with or without the use of moisture.

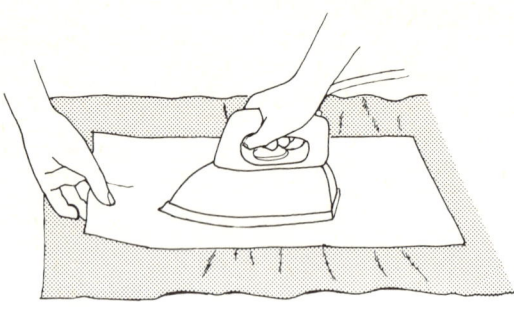

Figure 9

How much does it shrink?
1   Cut two identical pieces from your test piece.
2   Using the dry- or damp-press method press one piece all over.
3   Compare it with its twin to see if it has shrunk and if so, by how much?

Example   Tested sample piece reduced in size from 7.5 cm (3 in) by 7.5 cm (3 in) to 7 cm ($2\frac{3}{4}$ in) by 7 cm ($2\frac{3}{4}$ in). Therefore, 1 m (1 yd) will be reduced in size by 7.5 cm (3 in) in length and 7.5 cm (3 in) in width.

Pre-shrinking

If you have discovered, by using the previous test, that your fabric will shrink you will have to shrink it yourself before cutting out. Before doing this, however, you will need to know whether or not your fabric is washable.

WASHABLE FABRICS

If your fabric is washable then the following method is the simplest way of pre-shrinking the length:
1   Fold your length of fabric neatly to fit a washbowl or suitable container.
2   Half fill the container with water hot enough to wash your fabric.

3   Immerse your fabric in the water and allow it to cool.
4   Hang up in a suitable place to drip dry.
5   Press all over, if necessary, when dry.

NON-WASHABLE FABRICS—SHRINKING WITH MOISTURE

If you cannot wash your fabric then you will have to shrink it using moisture and heat in the following way:

1   Soak one half of your damp rag in water and wring it out on the other half.
2   Lay out your length of cloth, wrong side uppermost, on your press board allowing any excess length to rest comfortably on a chair beside the press board.
3   Starting at one end, lay the damp rag over the first section of your fabric.
4   With the iron controlled at the heat best suited to your cloth, press all over the damp rag covered section in an up-and-down motion until your damp rag is nearly dry.
5   Remove and re-moisten the damp rag and repeat the shrinking process section by section until you have shrunk the whole length of fabric.

Tailor's tips 11 and 12

11   A more manageable way of shrinking cloth is illustrated in Figure 10. This method may use more fabric than the pattern envelope states.

   1   Cut your garment from your cloth allowing extra seam allowances and hems around your pattern.
   2   Remove one section of the pattern at a time and shrink that section.
   3   When shrunk, replace the pattern and trim away excess fabric to desired size.

Note   Do not forget to shrink the larger offcuts; you may need them.

12   You may find that your local cleaner will steam press your garment length for you.

NON-WASHABLE FABRICS—SHRINKING WITHOUT MOISTURE

Fabrics that water mark and therefore need to be DRY PRESSED may also shrink under a hot iron. Follow the instructions for shrinking

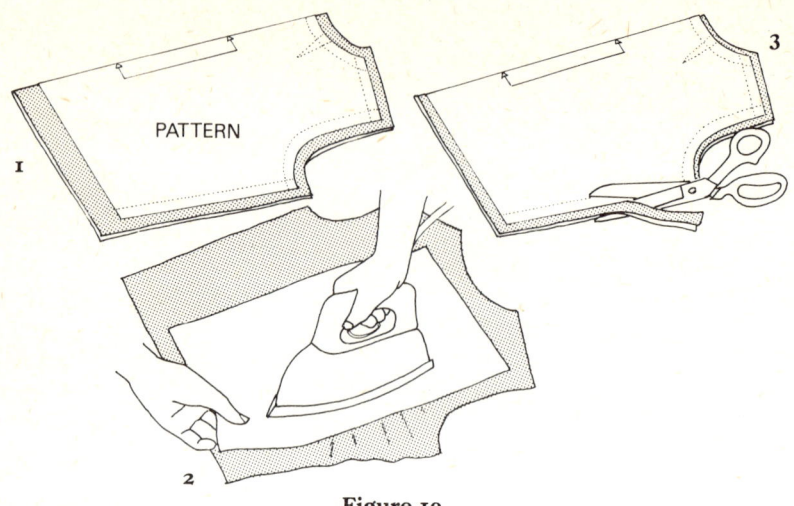

Figure 10

with moisture but substitute a dry press cloth for the damp rag. Tailor's tip **11** could easily be used here.

Remember Interfacings, braids, bindings, trimmings and piping cords may all shrink.

Test pressing seams and darts

1 Thread up your sewing machine and sew a seam and a dart in your test piece of fabric.
2 Whilst doing this check that you are using the correct sewing thread and machine needle and that the stitch length and tension are suitable for your fabric.
3 Make a note of these details for easy reference later.

THE DAMP-DABBER AND DAMP-RAG METHOD—SEAMS (Figure 11)

1 Bring forward the tailor's donkey on to the press board together with your moistened dabber and damp rag.
2 Preheat the iron to the correct temperature for your cloth and lay the unopened test seam, right sides together, along the donkey.
3 With the moistened dabber spread a thin film of water along the seam allowance.
4 Press the seam and, whilst still warm from the iron, open the seam and lay it face down along the donkey.

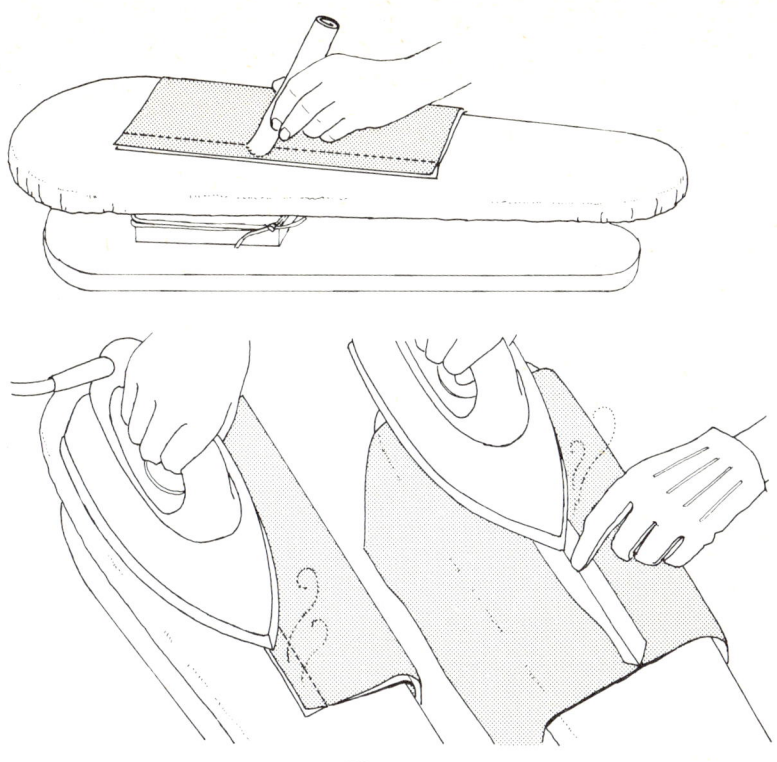

Figure 11

5   Spread another trace of moisture along the seam, opening the seam allowance as you go with your finger.

6   Following closely behind with the iron, press the seam open, coaxing it as you go with your gloved finger, or the dabber.

FIRMING SEAMS (Figure 12)

Finally, when you are sure that the seam has been pressed open properly and is not ridging to one side, the seam must be set. Tacks left in the seam can cause this ridged look. Be sure to remove them before doing any pressing. Inspect the right side as well as the underside for any fault and correct it, if necessary, by first pressing the now opened but ridged seam together and then carrying out the above instructions from no **4**.

To firm a seam proceed as follows:

1   Lay the opened seam, wrong side up, along the donkey.

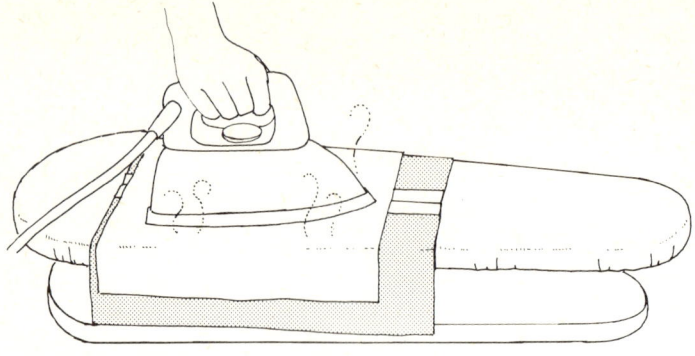

Figure 12

2   Place the damp rag over the opened seam and using an up-and-down motion, press with the iron gently but firmly all along the seam.

3   Remove the damp rag before it completely dries out and tap the excess steam out of the area with the tips of your fingers, the pounding block or the covered paperback book.

Tailor's tip 13

It may be necessary to increase the temperature of the iron when firming seams so that the heat will penetrate through the damp-rag on to the seam below. But always proceed with care.

THE DAMP-DABBER AND DAMP-RAG METHOD—DARTS (Figure 13)

1   Bring forward the tailor's ham and place it on top of the tailor's donkey.

2   Arrange the dart over one end of the ham, wrong side uppermost.

3   Spread a little moisture either side of the dart area and press either side of the dart close to the stitch-line. This should make the dart rise up.

4   Press the dart in the desired direction using an extra smear of moisture to help the dart to lie flat.

5   The bubbled effect often seen at dart ends can easily be shrunk away by pressing gently but firmly over the area, using the ham as a base. Care should, of course, be taken in sewing the dart to a very fine point before any pressing takes place.

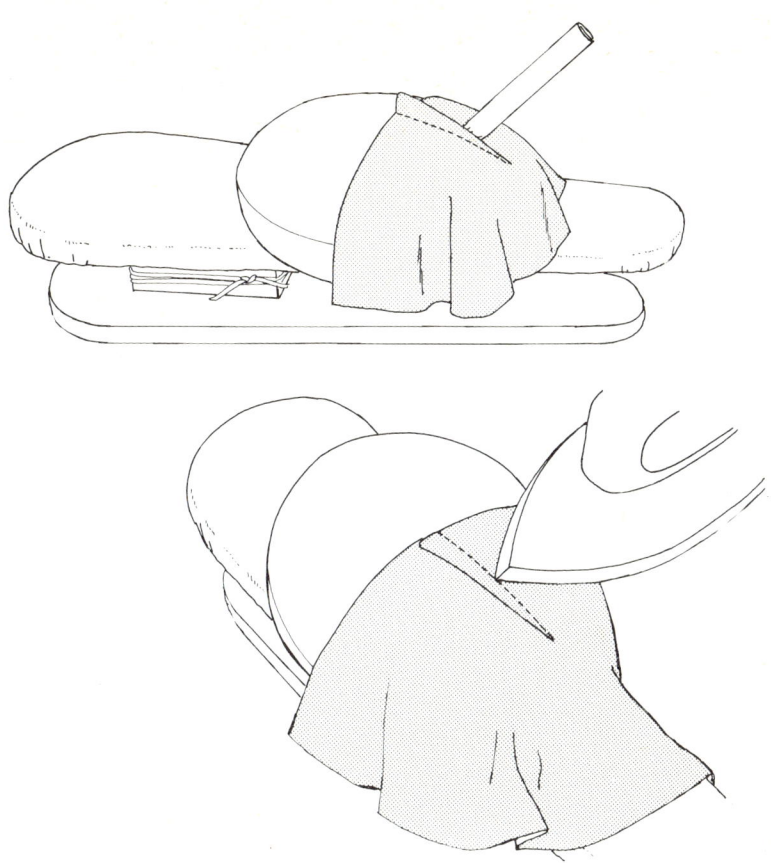

Figure 13

FIRMING DARTS

This process is carried out in the same manner as described for firming seams. Pay particular attention to the following points:

1   Make sure the tacks have been removed and there are no ridges on the right side of the dart.
2   Lay the dart over the part of the tailor's ham best suited to the curve of your dart.
3   Remove the damp-rag before it completely dries out.
4   If necessary use a heat setting slightly higher than when using the bare iron.

THE DRY-PRESS METHOD—FOR SEAMS THAT WATER MARK

1   Have you taken out those tacks?
2   Heat the iron to a suitable temperature and, laying the fabric on to the tailor's donkey, press the seam together with the bare iron.
3   Lay the seam on the donkey and coax the turnings open with your gloved finger, following closely behind with the tip of the bare iron.
4   Be careful not to create the ridged effect previously described.

THE DRY-PRESS METHOD—FOR DARTS THAT WATER MARK

The same technique is used for darts but substitute the tailor's ham, using the curved part of the ham best suited to the curve of your dart.

THE DAMP-DABBER AND DRY-PRESS METHOD

You may find that darts and seams in some fabrics will not press smoothly into place using the dry-press method. Even if your fabric water marks, it is possible with extreme care, to use the damp-dabber technique, making sure that only the tiniest smear of water is used and then only in the dart and seam area. Firm the seam or dart using the dry-press cloth technique.

Remember:

1   A dirty iron can cause irrevocable staining or singeing of your fabric. Always check that it is clean.
2   Too much moisture can cause as much damage as too hot an iron.
3   A damp rag is not a sopping wet cloth!
4   If you have finished dressmaking for the day hang your damp rag up to dry or it will develop an unpleasant odour. An occasional wash is a wise move.
5   It is always safer to press using a heat setting fractionally lower than the fabric can stand and allow the iron to rest a little longer on the area being pressed.
6   Your forefinger is an invaluable aid when coaxing seams open.
7   When pressing any seam open, it will press *open* much better if first you press the seam *together* using either the dabber or the dry-press method.
8   When firming a seam or dart, you may need a slightly higher

heat setting to penetrate through the protective press cloth on to the fabric underneath.

9 Some fabrics will need more coaxing, or need a harder or softer press surface than others. Experiment with all these suggestions in mind.

10 Mistakes in pressing can usually be corrected before too much heat is applied.

Phase 3
Under pressing

Under pressing is the term used for the first stage of pressing a garment and simply means pressing the seams and darts into their correct position on the wrong side of the fabric before they are crossed by other seams or before hems are turned up.

You have learnt the techniques of under pressing in the earlier chapter of testing and all that remains is to develop an organized approach to under pressing the garment as it is systematically put together.

Under pressing-as-you-go (Figure 14)

This does not mean that you sew a seam and then dash across to the press table to press it. It means getting into a routine of pressing a group of seams when you are ready to do so. You will be surprised how quickly you will get used to working in this way and how much easier it will be to attach one well-pressed section of your garment to another equally well-pressed part.

CURVED SEAMS AND DARTS (Figure 15)

Outer curves

These need to be clipped at regular intervals along the curve so that they will lie flat when pressed. Soft fabrics will only need a slight nick, stiffer fabrics will need a deeper nick into the seam allowances, every centimetre (half inch) or so to allow them to be pressed satisfactorily into place.

Inner curves

On stiff and heavy fabrics, to prevent seam allowances bunching together cut out notches at regular intervals along the seam allowance. On soft fabrics this will not be necessary.

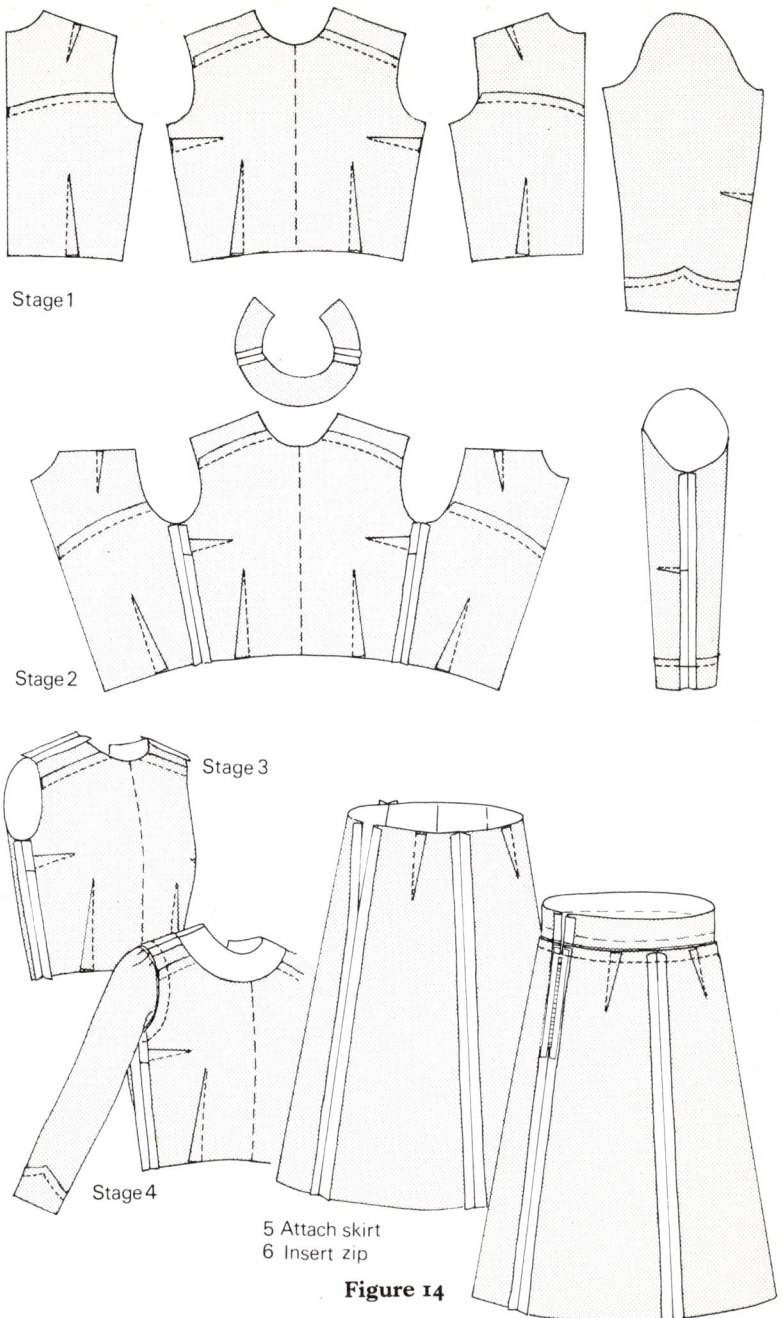

Stage 1

Stage 2

Stage 3

Stage 4

5 Attach skirt
6 Insert zip

Figure 14

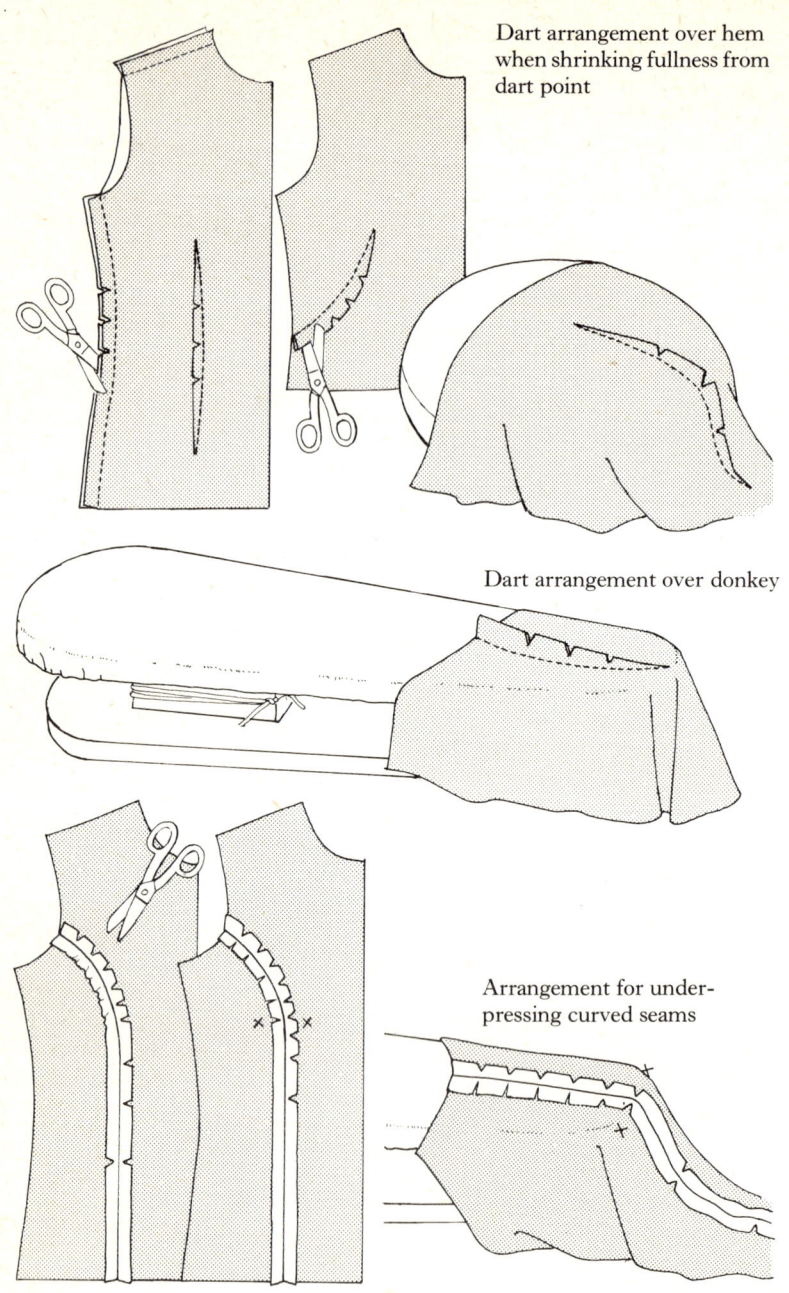

Figure 15

UNDERPRESSING A CURVED SEAM

Following the method best suited to your fabric:
1   Press the unopened seam right sides together.
2   Arrange and press open the seam as far as point **x** (the most curved part of the seam).
3   Turn the seam around and arrange and press open the second part.
4   Firm the seam in a similar manner.

GATHERED AREAS (Figure 16)
Yokes and sleeves
To reduce bulk in gathered yokes, sleeves, etc:
1   Arrange the area over a suitable press surface.
2   Press the seam allowance to flatten the gathered part. *Do not press* over the stitched line.

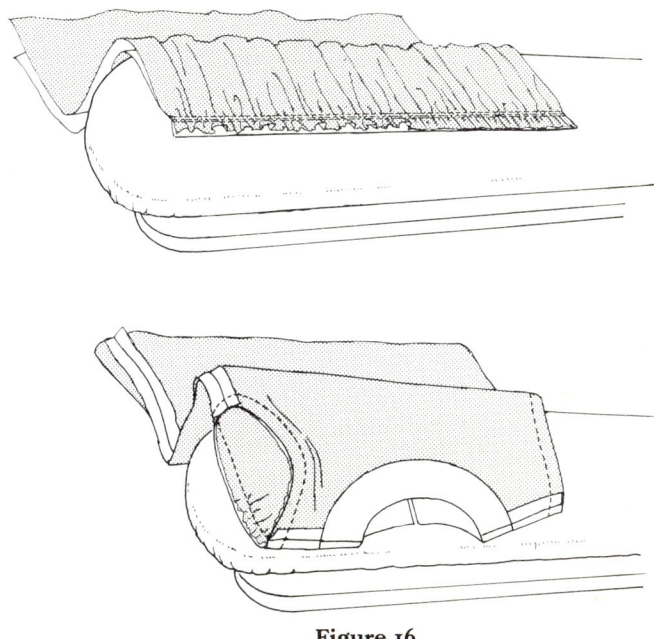

Figure 16

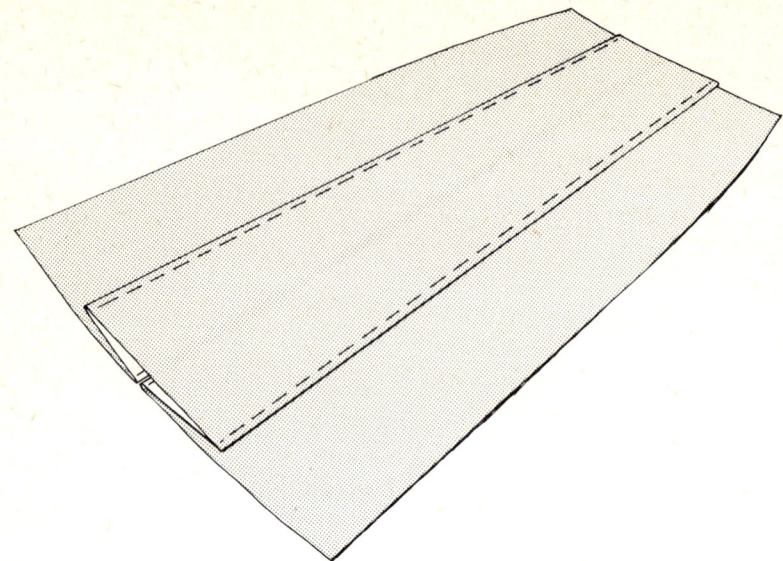

Figure 17

Figure 18

PLEATS AND DESIGN DETAIL (Figures 17 and 18)

For easy under pressing and complete control of pleats and other detail always arrange your work flat on the table and under press one section before attaching it to another.

PLAIN SLEEVE HEADS

Plain inset sleeves are best left to roll naturally over the armhole and sleeve seam allowances but a little under pressing will help them.

1   Arrange the sleeve and armhole over the end of the tailor's donkey and press them together on the wrong side, flattening the slightly gathered part of the sleeve head.

2   Gently press over the stitched seam line to shrink away any ease.

No other pressing should be needed.

Remember:

1   Tacks must be removed before under pressing seams and darts.
2   Press, do not stretch, seams open.
3   Experiment with different surfaces and thicknesses when pressing your garment.
4   Man-made sewing threads can suffer from too hot an iron just as much as man-made fabrics. Use a sewing thread suited to your fabric.
5   Pressing as you go means less final pressing and less possibility of unpicking necessitated by twisted seams.
6   It is easier to press a sleeve before it is set into a bodice, or a bodice before it is attached to a skirt, etc.
7   Keep a padded clothes hanger handy. Pin the pressed sections of your garment on it and hang them up until you are ready to use them.

Phase 4
Layering

Layering is the term used for thinning out seam allowances on collar edges, necklines, facings and front edges before they are turned out to the right side of the garment. Using sharp scissors, graduate the seam allowances as in Figure 19 to eliminate the unsightly thickness so often seen in badly made clothes.

Precise measurements are used in the examples given and generally speaking they are good guides to paring away excess turnings. However, the amount you trim away is dependent on how closely woven your fabric is and whether it frays badly, so please experiment.

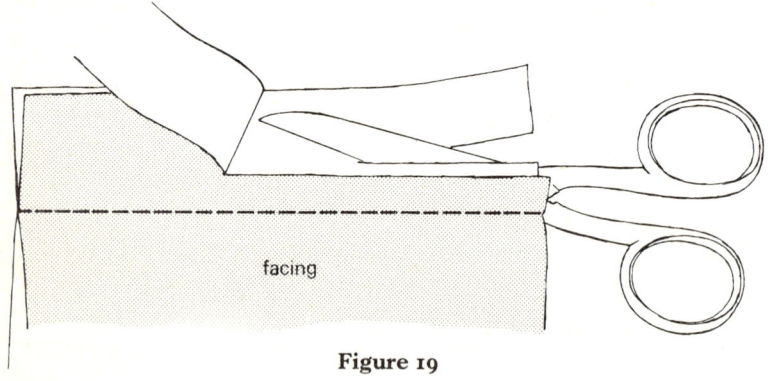

Figure 19

Hems (Figure 20)

Once you have decided on the length of your hem-line, trim away the seam allowances in the hem area to slightly less than those on the garment.

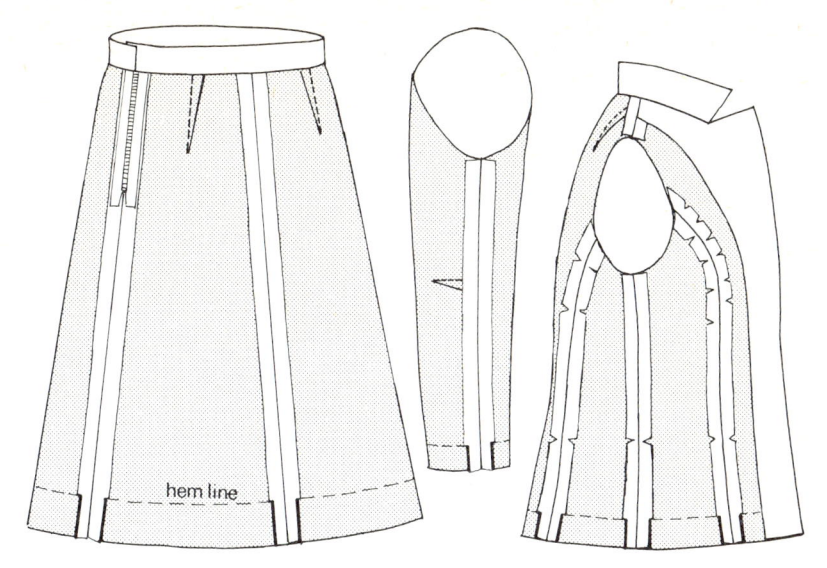

Figure 20

Example Seam allowances on garment: 16 mm ($\frac{5}{8}$ in).
Trim away 3 mm ($\frac{1}{8}$ in) from the hem seam allowances, leaving behind 13 mm ($\frac{1}{2}$ in) turning.

Even such a small amount will make all the difference when you turn up and press your hem-line.

Remember There are hem-lines on sleeves, jackets and blouses.

Necklines (Figure 21a)

Necklines will lie flatter and look much smoother if thoughtfully layered.
1   Trim away interfacing (if used) close to the stitch-line.
2   Trim away the seam allowance on your neckline leaving 6 mm ($\frac{1}{4}$ in).
3   On the facing of your neckline trim away slightly more, leaving only 4 mm ($\frac{3}{16}$ in).
4   If your neckline is square or angled you must clip into the corners close to the stitch line to allow your neckline to turn out satisfactorily. If round, clip all along the curve.

Figure 21

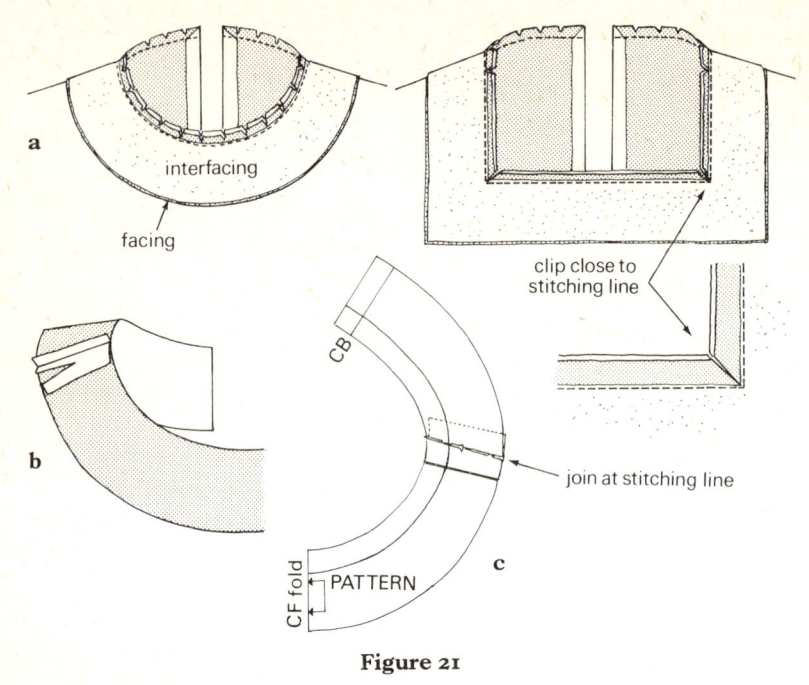

Neckline and sleeveless armhole facings (Figure 21b)

Trim away the seam allowance on these areas leaving behind 6 mm ($\frac{1}{4}$ in).

Tailor's tip 14 (Figure 21c)

In thicker fabrics bulk can be eliminated from these areas if you join these pattern sections together before cutting them out from your fabric.

1 Pin or stick the back and front facing patterns together, sewing line on sewing line.
2 Cut out the pattern section, now all in one, from your fabric, following the instructions on the front pattern section for 'straight of grain' placement line.
Note   It does not matter that the joined-on back section is 'off grain'.

Collars

Unless the outer edge of a collar is thinned it will not turn out well, and the thicker the fabric used the clumsier looking the edge will be. Collars are usually *interfaced*, which also adds to the thickness.

POINTED COLLARS (Figure 22)

1 Trim away the interfacing close to the stitch line.
2 Trim away all but 6 mm (¼ in) of the seam allowance on the *upper collar*.
3 Trim away all but 4 mm ($\frac{3}{16}$ in), i.e. slightly less, of the seam allowance on the *under collar*.
4 Cut across corners (pointed ends) of seam allowances leaving only 3 mm (⅛ in) turnings on the *upper* and *under collars*.

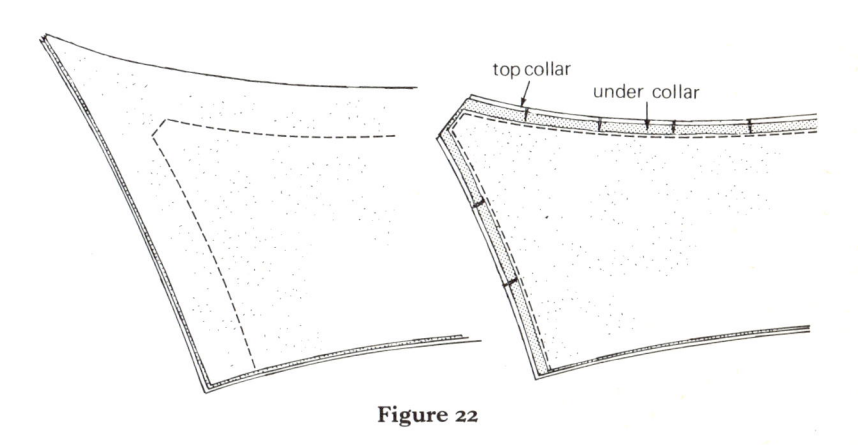

Figure 22

Tailor's tip 15

Your *pointed* collar will turn out looking much better if you machine stitch around your collar edge as follows:
1 Machine stitch along the sewing line of your collar to within 2 or 3 stitches of the corner.
2 Machine 2 or 3 stitches diagonally across the corner to reach the other edge.
3 Continue machine stitching along the second edge until the other collar point is all but reached (2 or 3 stitches) and repeat the process along the final edge.
Strange as it may seem, this blunting of the corner makes a sharper point when turned out to the right side, the reason being that the diagonal stitches allow the turnings more room to lie flat.

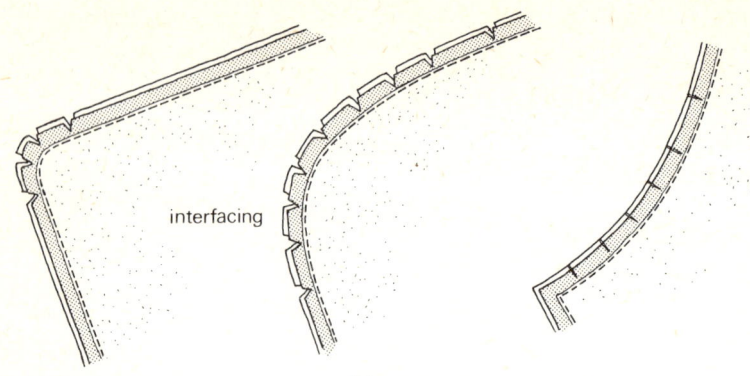

Figure 23

Rounded collars (Figure 23)
1   Trim away the interfacing close to the stitch-line.
2   Trim away all but 6 mm ($\frac{1}{4}$ in) of the seam allowance on the *upper collar*.
3   Trim away all but 4 mm ($\frac{3}{16}$ in), i.e. slightly less, of the seam allowance on the *under collar*.

Tailor's tip 16
On the very *rounded* parts of the collar's outer edge, especially with medium and heavy-weight fabrics, cut out notches from what is left of the seam allowances to reduced bunching of the allowances when the collar is turned out to the right side.

Remember:
1   The interfacing is always trimmed back to the stitched line.
2   The edge which will be uppermost in the finished garment is always the one with the largest amount of turning.
Example   Upper collar—trimmed back to 6 mm ($\frac{1}{4}$ in).
Under collar—trimmed back to 4 mm ($\frac{3}{16}$ in).

Lapels and front edges (Figure 24)
Following the above rules, layering on lapels and front edges is carried out in two sections:

Figure 24

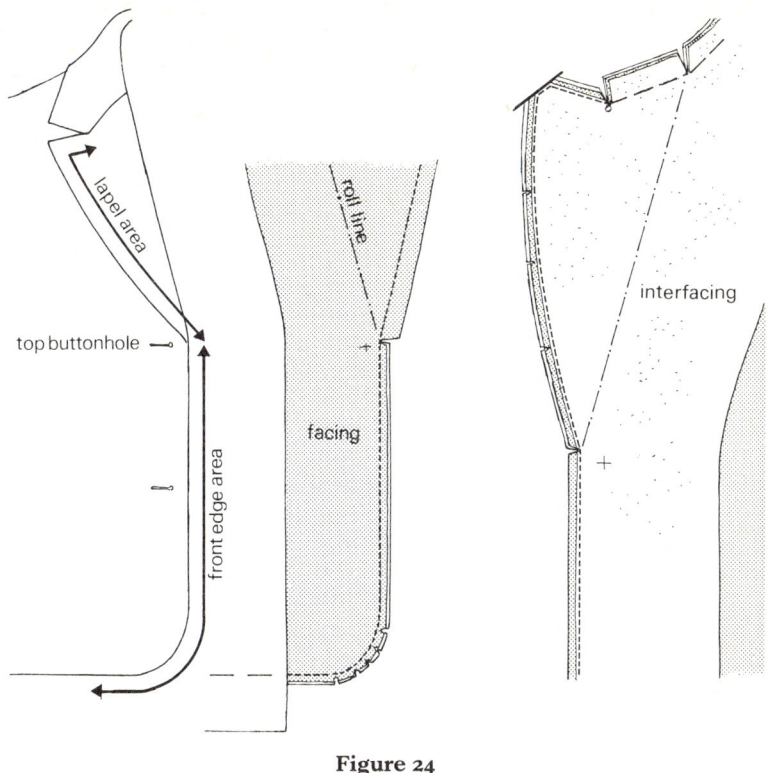

FRONT EDGE AREA

1   Trim away the seam allowance to all by 6 mm ($\frac{1}{4}$ in) on the front edge seam.
2   Trim away the seam allowance to all but 4 mm ($\frac{3}{16}$ in), i.e. slightly less, on the front edge facing.

LAPEL AREA

1   Reversing the procedure, trim away the seam allowance to all but 6 mm ($\frac{1}{4}$ in) on the *lapel facing*.
2   Trim away all but 4 mm ($\frac{3}{16}$ in) (slightly less) on the *lapel* which is a continuation of the *upper front edge*.

Use the previous tailor's tip **15** when sewing the corners of your lapels.

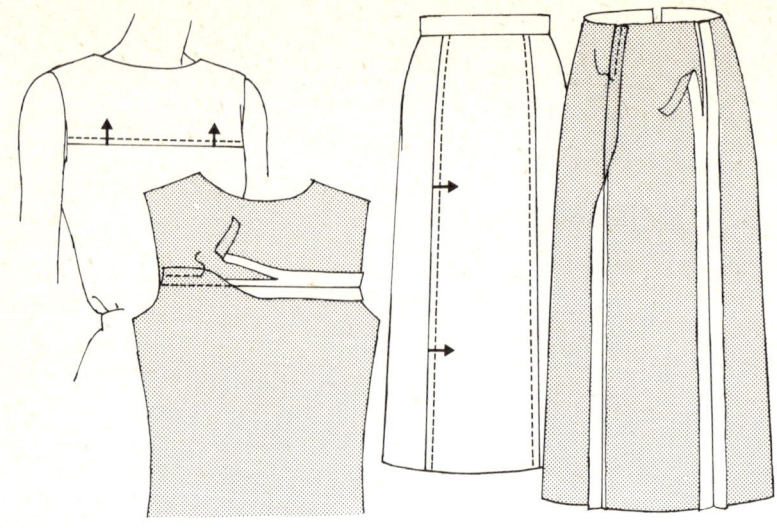

Figure 25

Layering seams before top stitching (Figure 25)

Decorative machine or hand top stitching is much easier to achieve if one of the seam allowances is pared away beforehand so that the top stitching has only to penetrate through two thicknesses instead of three. It is also easier to machine stitch whilst your garment is in sections.

1   Decide which way your seam is to lie.
2   Trim away the inner seam (the one that doesn't show) to less than the desired width of top stitching.
3   Tack the seam down along the top-stitching line on the right side of the garment.
4   Machine or hand top stitch comfortably through *two* instead of *three* thicknesses.

Using the iron when layering edges (Figure 26)

1   Edges will turn out to the right side much more easily if you first of all press them together.
Remember to use the pressing technique best suited to your fabric.
2   On medium and heavy-weight fabrics, after pressing the edges together, coax open the seam slightly with the tip of your iron to ensure a nicely turned out facing, collar or neckline.

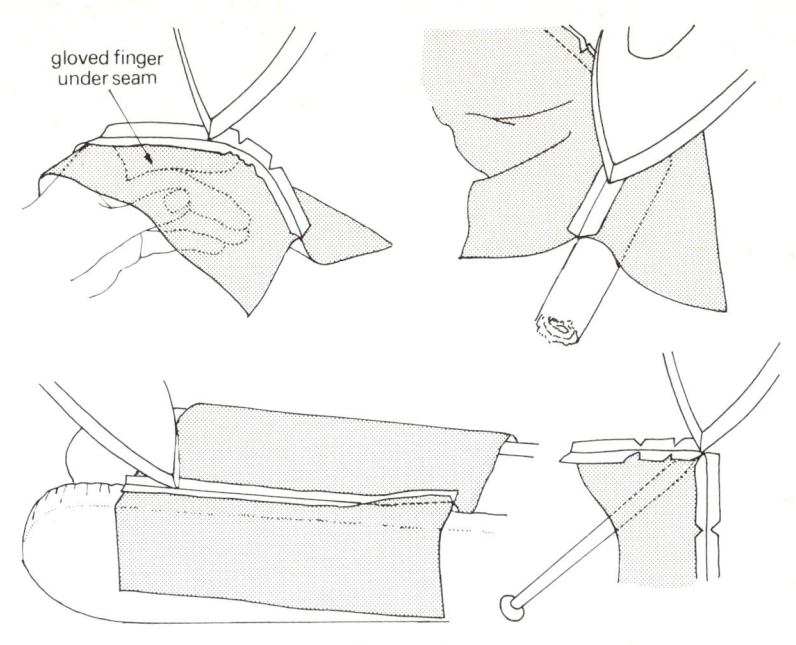

Figure 26

a Support the seam on your gloved finger, the small press pad, the edge of your dabber or the edge of the tailor's donkey laid on its side.
b If applicable, apply a minuscule amount of water to the seam and coax it open with the tip of your iron.
c If you cannot use moisture, coax the seam open with the dry, bare iron.
d Remember you are only coaxing the seam open slightly and not trying to open it flat. Be careful not to stretch the seams.

Layering iron-on interfacings

If an iron-on interfacing is used in the areas previously mentioned it will be impossible to trim the interfacing close to the stitch line once it is stuck to the fabric. To overcome this problem:

1 Cut the interfacing to shape and tack it on to the pieces requiring interfacing such as the neck-edge, facing, collar.
2 Machine stitch around the facing, collar, neck-edge etc.

3 Trim away the interfacing close to the stitch-line.

4 Remove the tacking, then press the iron-on interfacing all over the area.

On closely woven or firm materials the following alternative method could be used:

1 Cut iron-on interfacing without seam allowances.

2 Place iron-on interfacing carefully on the part to be interfaced and press it on.

3 Use the interfacing edge as a sewing-line guide.

Phase 5
Top pressing

Top pressing is the term used for pressing hems, collar edges, necklines and facings into their correct position. If you have carefully followed the techniques on UNDER PRESSING and LAYERING you will discover how much easier TOP PRESSING becomes and how much more professional your garment will look.

Before top pressing

It is much easier to get a smooth looking edge to your collar, facing, hem or neckline if you tack the edge into position after turning these parts of the garment out to the right side. Here, again, you will realize how much simpler this is once you have used the layering technique.

There is always the possibility of tack impressions remaining after pressing but these are easily removed when you finally *Press off* your garment.

A protective press cloth

For the first time you will be pressing on the right side of your fabric and its surface needs to be protected from the iron with a protective press cloth as well as a DAMP or DRY PRESS CLOTH, depending on how your fabric responds to heat and moisture.

This press cloth could be the piece of woollen worsted, the piece of pure silk or cotton twill, or the spare test piece. Your choice will depend on the pressing method used.

1   The woollen worsted or the piece of itself will be best suited to damp-pressing.
2   The piece of pure silk or cotton twill, or the piece of itself should be chosen when dry-pressing.

3   Any of these protective press cloths could be used for the damp-dabber and dry-press method.

Tailor's tip 17

When tacking your edges (*basting out*) the use of a soft basting cotton in place of harder sewing threads will help prevent tack impressions remaining in the fabric.

Press surfaces

Experiment with your press aids until you find the one that suits the part you are pressing.
1   Hems will need quite a large area. Use your press board and press banket folded into a suitable thickness.
2   To press inside a neckline try the tailor's ham.
3   To press a trouser hem or sleeve cuff try inserting the paperback book or press pad inside.
4   The press roll can be used in all sorts of awkward areas.

Tailor's tip 18

On garments made from *medium* to *heavy* fabrics lightly rub a piece of dampened household soap along the wrong side of hem lines and edges before turning them in to their finished position. When top pressing them the slightly adhesive properties of the soap will give your edge or hem a sharper finish. Try this method on trouser creases.

Methods of top pressing

Top pressing is carried out on the underside of the garment. That is to say, the right side of the fabric but on that part of the garment that doesn't show when worn.

Top pressing with a damp rag

1   Protect the edge to be pressed with a suitable protective press cloth.
2   Lay your moistened damp rag ($\frac{1}{4}$ wet wrung out on $\frac{3}{4}$ dry) on top of the protective press cloth.
3   With the iron heated to a suitable temperature press through both cloths to introduce steam into the edge.
4   Remove your damp rag and firm the edge through the protective press cloth.

Top pressing with dry press cloths

Use this method for materials that are affected by moisture.

1 Lay your protective press cloth, folded double, over the edge to be pressed.
2 With the iron set at a suitable temperature, press the edge with a firm up and down motion.
3 Finally press the edge through one thickness of protective press cloth.

Top pressing with dry press cloths and damp dabber

It is possible to apply a little moisture to help in coaxing stubborn edges into place even when the fabric is affected by moisture, but please take care.

1 Protect the edge to be pressed with your chosen protective press cloth folded double.
2 Apply the tiniest trace of moisture to the edge area only, using the dabber.
3 Press the area through both thicknesses, remove one fold of the press cloth and firm the edge through the remaining fold.

Example 1 : jacket (Figure 27)

Use the following sequence for top pressing a jacket:

1 Insert the paperback book inside the sleeve hems and press them on the right side (narrow openings are pressed easiest from the right side).
2 Lay the jacket on the press table right side down, inner side upwards.
3 Starting at the centre back hem, top press along the hem and up the front edges finishing at the top button and button-hole.
4 Allow the pressed section to rest on the press board until dry (a few seconds). Remove and reverse the jacket, wrong side down, with the under collar towards you.
5 Starting at the centre back under collar, top press in either direction down each side of the under collar and lapel until the top button and button-hole are reached.
6 Hang up the garment to dry off.

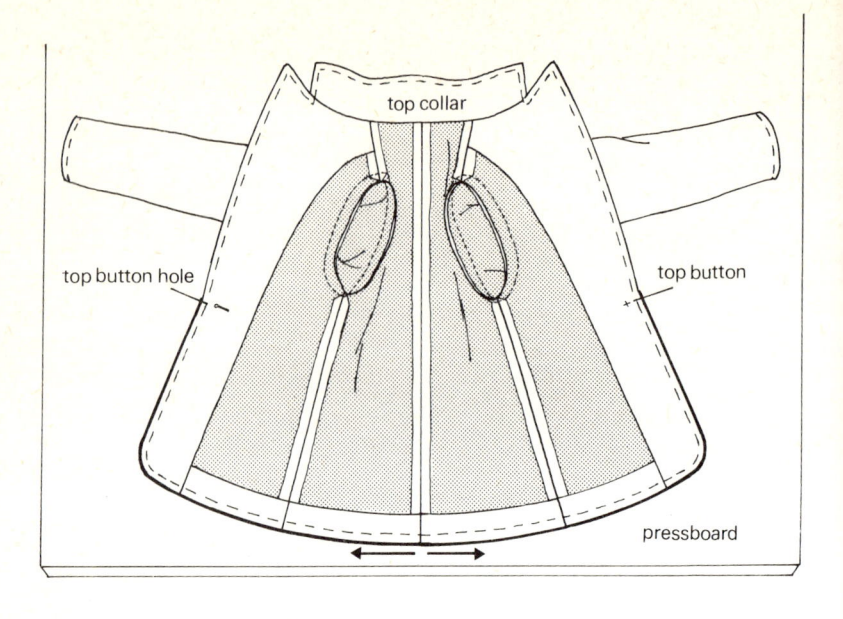

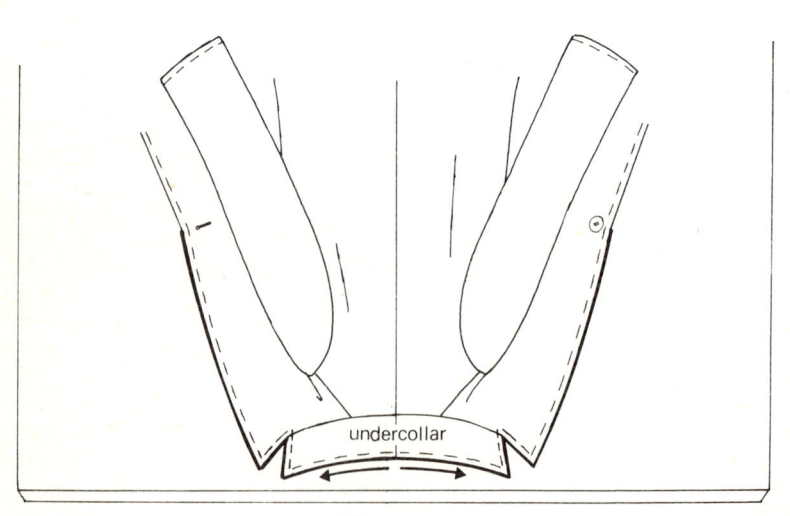

Figure 27

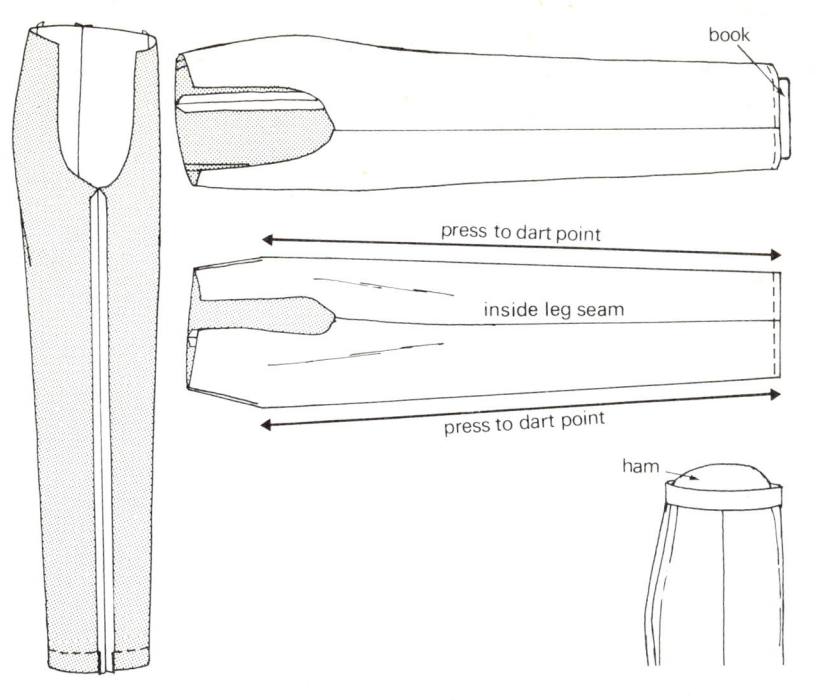

Figure 28

Example 2 : trousers (Figure 28)
The following is the sequence for under pressing and top pressing trousers as you go. Trousers are much easier to make and press if each leg is kept separate for as long as possible.
1   Under press each leg.
2   Tack the crotch seams together and tack the waist band whilst fitting and establishing the right length.
3   Top press the hems from the right side (insert paperback book).
4   Top press the creases into place.
5   Finally join the crotch seam, sew in the zip fastener and attach the waistband.
6   Press off with all tacks removed. Insert the tailor's ham inside the waist band to press off that area.

Phase 6
Pressing off

At last you have finished your garment! Strange as it may seem, there is very little final pressing to do, that is if you have carried out carefully the various stages described in this book.

Pressing off is a continuation of top pressing and simply means top pressing the hems and edges of your garment for a second time to *firm* and *set* these parts and to remove any impressions caused by tacks or pins. Should any other parts need pressing, and they should be minimal if you have carried out each stage with care, try inserting your tailor's ham or other suitable press aid inside the garment to support the area to be top pressed and follow the top pressing instruction best suited to your fabric.

The final press

The final press is carried out on the right side of the garment, that is to say the parts of the garment that show when worn.

1   Remove all tacks and pins.
2   Lay a protective press cloth over the area to be pressed off.
3   Firmly but gently press over the extreme edges of the garment using the damp or dry method best suited to your fabric.
4   Follow the top pressing sequence but on the *right side* of the garment.

Hanging up and drying off

Hanging a section of garment or the whole garment up to dry off is mentioned several times in this book. It must be stressed that at no time should your garment be *wet*. *Hanging up* and *drying off* simply means allowing the humidity to disperse before handling the garment further and lessens the risk of stretching or creasing the fabric.

Phase 7
Difficult and Unusual Fabrics

It cannot be stressed strongly enough that testing is the basis on which to build up confidence in handling a piece of fabric. Most fabrics however unusual or strange will usually respond to one of the methods described in the chapter on testing. The exceptions are fabrics that have a pile or napped surface.

These fabrics have two things in common:

1 The sections of the garment must be cut in one direction to prevent shading.
2 They all need pressing with steamy damp rags to prevent the pile or napped surface from being bruised by the iron.

Pile fabrics

Pile fabrics come in a variety of weights and textures from the heaviest of velour cloth down to the thinnest of velvets with a range of camel hair, cashmere, velveteen and needlecord in between.

Paradoxically, although they all bruise easily they all press much better on top of a hard surface. They divide easily into two types:

1 *Napped surface* or *short pile*: velour, camel hair, etc.
2 *Long pile*: velvet, corduroys, etc.

PRESSING

The 'hiss and steam method' is used for both types of pile fabric with one important difference when pressing:

1 *Short pile fabrics*: the iron presses gently but firmly on the damp rag.
2 *Long pile fabrics*: the iron *never* presses on the damp rag but *hovers* just above it

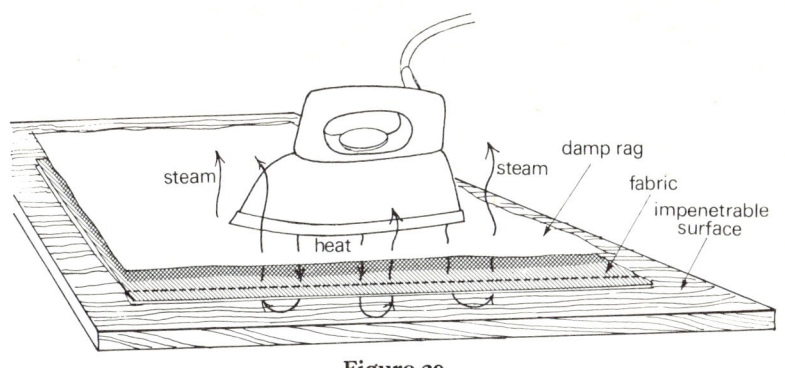

Figure 29

The 'hiss and steam' method (Figure 29)
On contact with the damp rag the hot iron causes steam to penetrate through the fabric onto the impenetrable, wooden surface below; the steam bounces back through the fabric leaving the area malleable enough to arrange into its correct position.

Tailor's tip 19

Your velvet, needlecord or velveteen garment will have a much richer look if you cut all the sections of the garment with the pile running *upwards*.

Short pile fabrics

Pressing surface: Could be the wooden underside of the tailor's donkey, or the bare wood of the pressboard, or the pressboard with one layer of press blanket, the uncovered cardboard roll or the tailor's ham covered with paper.

Damp rag: Should be wetter than for plain fabrics. Soak $\frac{3}{4}$ and wring out on $\frac{1}{4}$.

Dabber: Should be well soaked but not dripping wet

Iron: Should be hot enough to 'hiss and steam' on contact with the damp rag.

SEAMS

Under pressing
1 Have you remembered to take your tacks out?
2 Lay the unopened seam, right sides together, along the wooden underside of your tailor's donkey or other such hard surface.

3   Lay your damp rag on top of the seam and press gently but firmly, allowing the steam to penetrate to the seam.

4   Whilst still warm and steamy, arrange the seam along the hard surface, right side down, seam uppermost.

5   With your prepared dabber in one hand and the iron in the other, place the tip of your iron on to the soaked end of your dabber so as to cause steam to emerge from the dabber.

6   Pass the steaming dabber along the seam coaxing it open as you go.

Firming

1   After coaxing open the seam with the steamy dabber lay your damp rag, folded double, over the opened seam.

2   Press all along the seam gently but firmly and remove the damp rag whilst still steamy.

3   Gently brush out the excess steam in the direction of the pile with a clothes brush.

4   Hang up each section as soon as you have firmed it so that it dries off, otherwise you may crush the pile surface.

DARTS (Figure 30)

Darts in pile fabrics, and indeed in very heavy or thick fabrics, are best cut and pressed open. This is possible on all darts that are bigger than 12 mm ($\frac{1}{2}$ in) in width. Consideration must be given to the tendency of the cloth to fray and care taken when slitting down the dart.

1   With sharp scissors slit down the fold of the sewn dart.
2   Overcast or machine zigzag the slit.

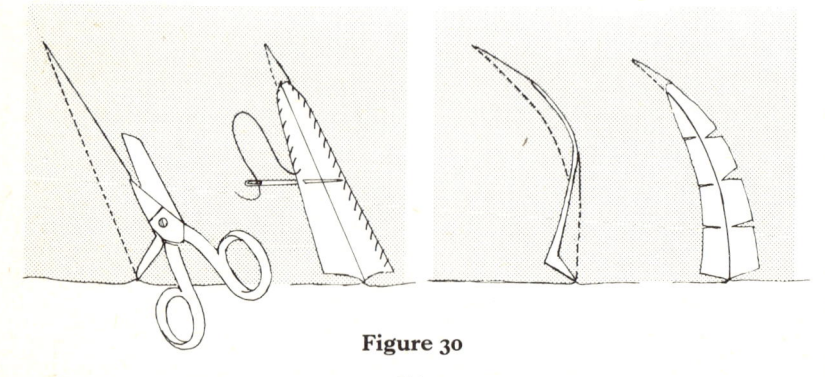

Figure 30

Figure 31

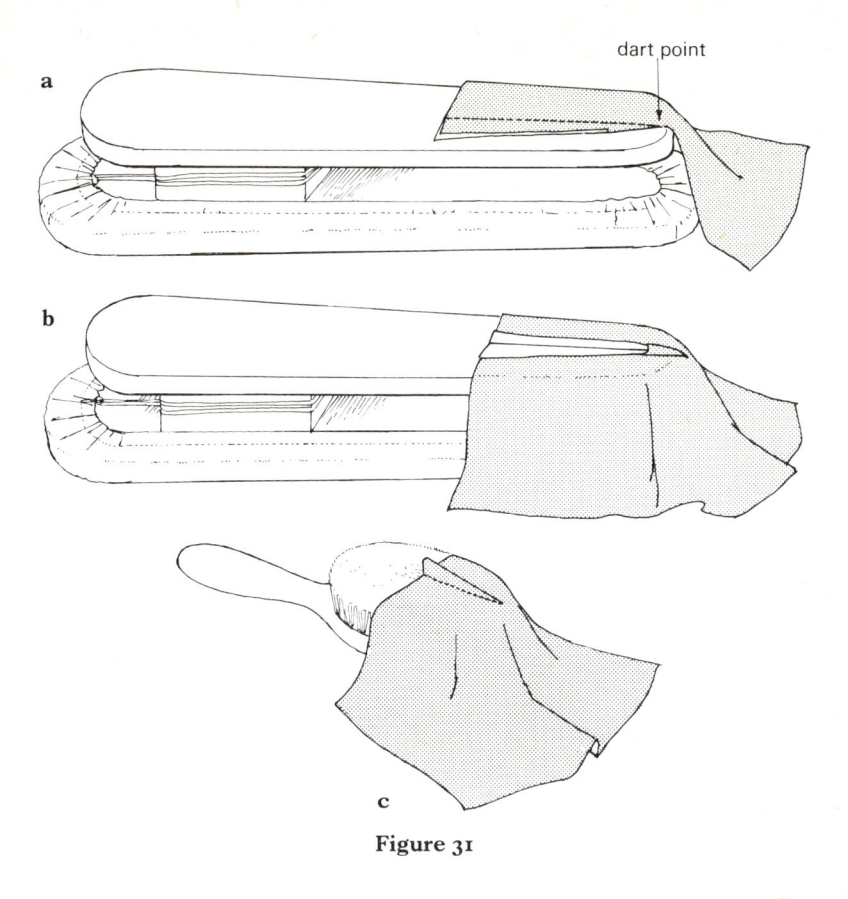

CUT AND OPENED DARTS (Figure 31a and b)

Under pressing

1 Lay the cut, but unopened, dart along one end of the wooden underside of your tailor's donkey, dart uppermost.
2 Place your damp rag on top of, but not beyond, the point of the dart.
3 Press along the dart as far as its point.
4 Arrange the still warm and damp dart over the end of your donkey, right side down, dart uppermost, with the point of the dart just over the end of the donkey.
5 Using the steaming dabber and hot iron method coax open the dart.

Firming

1   Lay your coaxed open dart over a suitable curve on your tailor's ham, dart uppermost.
2   Lay your damp rag folded in two on top of the dart and gently but firmly press over the dart area.
3   Remove the damp rag and brush out the excess steam with a clothes brush. Hang each section up to dry as soon as you have firmed it.

SMALL DARTS (Figure 31c)

Small darts that cannot be cut and pressed open can be pressed over the bristles of a clothes brush.

1   Lay the small dart over the bristles of a clothes brush, dart uppermost right side of fabric (pile) sinking into the bristles.
2   Lay your damp rag, folded double, over the dart and press the area.
3   Remove the damp rag and shake or brush out the excess steam. No firming is needed.

TOP PRESSING

1   Remember to layer all your hems and edges.
2   Lay the hem or edge to be top pressed on to a suitable surface, right side down.
3   Cover the edge to be pressed with a protective press cloth. This could be a piece of the material itself face down.
4   Lay your damp rag on top of the protective press cloth and press gently but firmly all along the hem or edge area through both cloths.
5   Remove both cloths whilst still steamy and brush out the excess steam with a clothes brush in the direction of the pile.
6   Hang up until dry.

WATER MARKING ON SHORT PILE FABRICS

Short pile fabrics quite often need to be pressed all over with a steamy damp rag to remove the surface patina or sheen which remains on the unpressed areas of the garment, giving the garment a blotchy or mottled look. Tailor's tip 11, on page 23, is the most successful method of removing this sheen and can be used even though your fabric does not require shrinking.

Long-pile fabrics—velvet and velvet types

USE OF THE IRON

When under pressing and firming seams and darts follow closely the techniques used for pile fabrics with one important exception. Instead of pressing firmly but gently, hover the iron close enough to the damp rag to cause it to 'hiss and steam' so that the steam penetrates through to the seam or dart below. On no account allow your iron to rest on velvet or velvet types.

TOP PRESSING

1 Lay a prepared damp rag, folded double, on top of a hard surface.
2 Lay the hem or edge to be pressed on top of the double damp rag, right side down, hem or inner edge uppermost.
3 Lay a second damp rag, folded double, on top of the area to be pressed.
4 With your iron hot enough to 'hiss and steam' the damp rag, *hover* your iron close enough to cause steam to penetrate through to the hem or edge below.
5 Remove the top damp rag and brush out the excess steam.
6 Hang the garment up until dry.

Heavy fabric

Very heavy or thick fabrics can be troublesome when trying to press seam allowances flat. A steamy damp rag and a firm surface can be helpful. Lingering longer with the iron can sometimes be the answer. Banging out the excess steam with the pounding block can often help. Please experiment and do layer your edges, cut and press open the darts and clip the seam allowances.

Very thin fabrics

Very thin fabrics of a brittle nature can quite often be unresponsive to a medium-hot iron, yet raising the heat control results in burnt or shrivelled fabric. It is wise to consider what kind of garment is best made from this type of fabric and what type of seams will be most suitable. The simplified shirt seam, described on page 59, can be used with this type of fabric.

Knitted or non-woven fabrics

One difficulty that can arise when sewing with knitted or non-woven fabrics is that seam allowances tend to curl up when pressed open and will not be coaxed into place. Rethinking the method of sewing seams used with these fabrics could be the answer to this problem. The simplified shirt seam, described on page 59, is suitable for knitted or non-woven fabrics.

ALTERNATIVE SEAMS—for brittle, knitted or non-woven fabrics

Garments made from very thin, brittle fabrics or from knitted or non-woven fabrics often fall in folds or are worn loose. To overcome the problems that arise when pressing these fabrics use one of the following methods:

1 Press the seam allowances together and allow them to fall naturally.

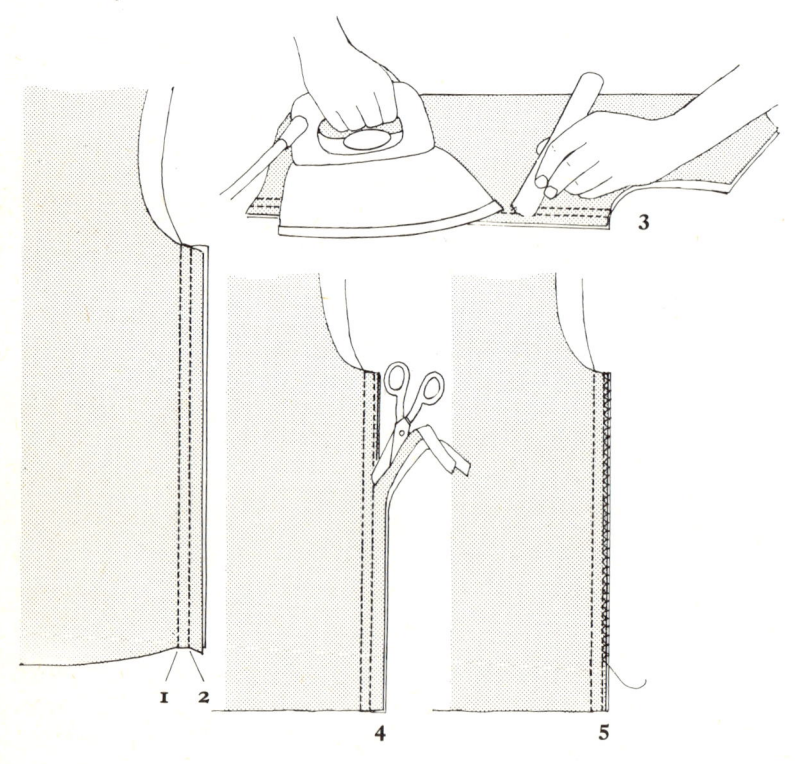

Figure 32

2 Secure the seam allowances to one side or the other with decorative top-stitching.
3 Use the simplified version of the seam so often used in shirt factories nowadays (see below).

Simplified shirt seam (Figure 32)
1 Machine stitch the seam in the usual way along the sewing line with the right sides of the fabric together.
2 Machine stitch a second row 6 mm ($\frac{1}{4}$ in) away from the first row of stitching on the seam allowance.
3 At this stage try to press the seam together, using a damp dabber if possible.
4 Trim away the excess seam allowance close to the second row of machine stitching.
5 Zigzag over the second row of machine stitching.

Tailor's tips 20–22

20 When *removing tacks* from velvet avoid marking the pile by cutting through each tack stitch and pulling each section of tack out separately and vertically.

21 *Steam pressing* (Figure 33): This tip is very useful for reviving old or creased clothes in a variety of fabrics and textures, and is particularly good for velvet and velvet types.
    1 Arrange the finished garment on a dress stand, clothes hanger or the back of a chair, conveniently near to a suitable electric point.
    2 Half fill an electric kettle and switch it on to boil.
    3 Place your cardboard press roll over the kettle's spout.
    4 When steam emerges from the press roll direct it on to the garment. *Wear gloves* to avoid burning yourself.
    5 Brush the steam into and out of the fabric in the direction of the pile.
    6 Switch off your kettle periodically or you will create too much steam. *Do not* allow your kettle to boil dry.

22 To give *fur fabrics* a more realistic appearance, seams can quite often be hidden by:
    1 Easing out the pile that has been caught into the seam or dart when it was sewn, with a thick needle or bodkin.
    2 Under pressing and brushing the pile well.

Figure 33

Remember:
1   Gloved fingers will protect your hands from steam.
2   Your edges will not press well unless layered.
3   Pile fabrics will crush if not hung up and allowed to dry.
4   The iron *hovers* and *never rests* on velvet and velvet-type fabrics.
5   Velvet-type fabrics, once firmed cannot be unpressed.
6   Soft basting cotton is better for tacking than hard sewing threads.
7   When pressing pile fabrics the damp rag should never be allowed to dry out.
8   Simple styles and special seams can often solve problems with unresponsive materials.

Tailor's tip 23
Finally, it is my experience that seam impressions showing through to the right side of the garment and permanent impressions made by tacking cotton on the fabric are caused by:
1 Too hot an iron.
2 Far too wet a damp rag.

Phase 8
Other uses for press aids

The simple press aids that are used in this book can often be used as supports when pinning, tacking or hand sewing the garment you are making. Hand sewing can be therapeutic until one finds that one has accidentally sewn one section on to another. Why not relax in a comfortable chair with your tailor's ham on your knees, separating and raising up the part you are sewing?

The wooden underside of your tailor's donkey can be used to separate and raise up one part of a skirt thus isolating the part you are working on.

The paperback book or small press pad can be used to insert inside narrower parts such as sleeves, cuffs and other such areas.

Tailor's ham

Use the tailor's ham to separate and support:

1 your bodice when pinning and sewing on braid, lace or other trimmings.
2 the neck area when re-designing a neck-line or shaping a yoke.
3 the same area when cutting a facing pattern for the re-designed neckline.
4 the bodice or hip area when pinning on pockets.
5 the neck area when arranging collars.
6 when pinning linings into garments.

Keep your tailor's ham handy on washday, it can be invaluable as a support when ironing difficult areas in your laundry, and so useful when pressing your washed woollies.

Tailor's donkey

Use the wooden underside of the tailor's donkey to separate and support:
1 when pinning trimmings on to large areas such as hems.
2 the front edges of coats and jackets when arranging detail.
3 when pinning in linings in skirts.
4 front edges for easier button placement.
5 when arranging pleats or folds in skirts.